WALKING WITH PURPOSE
DISCUSSION QUESTIONS

FIRST EDITION

Copyright © 2013 Lisa Brenninkmeyer

Published by Beacon Publishing.

Book Cover Design by:

Jillian Buhl • Melissa Overmyer • Allison Taylor

For more information on this title and other books and CDs
available through the Dynamic Catholic Book Program,
please visit: www.DynamicCatholic.com

The Dynamic Catholic Institute

2200 Arbor Tech Drive

Hebron, KY 41048

Phone 1-859-980-7900

Email: info@DynamicCatholic.com

Printed in the United States of America.

Table of Contents

I want to live purposefully. I want to give my time to the things that truly matter. Even with all my good intentions, there are nights when I lie awake, filled with regret over choices I've made, or nervousness about what the next day will bring. Sometimes I get a little worn out from trying so hard. Other times I'm not quite sure where to start. The mountain seems high, and I have a hard time breaking down the big goal (purposeful living!) into doable steps. This study guide is meant to break down some of the big topics in the book into discussion questions that lead to action steps. You can go through this study guide on your own, or better yet, get some friends together and do it in a group setting. It's such an encouragement to know you're not alone, your struggles are shared, and your victories are celebrated!

SESSION

1

PUTTING SOME BASICS IN PLACE

Read the Introduction and
Section One: Putting Some Basics in Place

> Many things get in the way of our really believing that God loves us. We tend to attribute to God the characteristics of our earthly fathers. If your father wasn't loving, you may find it hard to believe that your Heavenly Father loves you unconditionally.
> —*Walking with Purpose*, page 13

1. George MacDonald offered the following advice for those whose negative experiences of an earthly father was harming their ability to receive God's fatherly love: "You must interpret the word by all that you have missed in life." What do the following verses reveal about our Heavenly Father? *Record your thoughts on the next page.*

Psalm 91:4, "He will shelter you with his pinions, and under his wings you may take refuge; his faithfulness is a protecting shield."

Psalm 145:8, "The LORD is gracious and merciful, slow to anger and abounding in mercy."

> "Whatever you have done, whatever you've become, it doesn't matter. Please come home and discover God's love for you." There is no sin greater than God's mercy.
> —*Walking with Purpose,* page 16

2. What do the following verses promise about God's limitless mercy?

Lamentations 3:22-23, "The Lord's acts of mercy are not exhausted, his compassion is not spent; they are renewed each morning- great is your faithfulness."

Isaiah 1:18, "Come now, let us set things right, says the LORD; Though your sins be like scarlet, they may become white as snow; though they be red like crimson, they may become white as wool."

1 John 1:9, "If we acknowledge our sins, he is faithful and just and will forgive our sins and cleanse us from every wrongdoing."

3. *"Essential #2: Recognizing What Drives You"* (page 16) explored three common motivators that can affect our behavior. Which of these motivations (pride, vanity, people pleasing) best describes you? It's likely that all three describe you at certain times, but one should describe you more consistently.

4. In order to stop seeking security in the wrong places, we need to develop the virtues and strengths that are the opposite of our vices and weaknesses. Circle the virtue below that best describes where you want to grow. Read the Bible verse that corresponds to that virtue, then record a concrete step you can take this week to develop faith, hope or love.

Faith (to counter pride)

Proverbs 3:5, "Trust in the Lord with all your heart and lean not on your own understanding. In all your ways, acknowledge him, and he will make your paths straight."

Hope (to counter sensuality)

2 Corinthians 4:16-18, "So we do not lose heart, though our outer self is wasting away, our inner self is being renewed day by day. For this light momentary affliction is preparing for us an eternal weight of glory beyond all comparison, as we look not to the things that are seen but to the things that are unseen. For the things that are seen are transient, but the things that are unseen are eternal."

Love (to counter people pleasing)

1 John 4:18, "There is no fear in love, but perfect love drives out fear."

Notes

5. In order to decrease distractions and do the things that are most important to us, it's helpful to look at our daily schedules and record where all the time goes. Take a day and record your activities as you go. The following day, take some time to reflect on why you chose those activities. What were your motivations? Did any of your activities have eternal value?

Record any insights below.

Notes

6. We read in Mark 1:35 Jesus rose before dawn, he "went off to a deserted place, where he prayed." Each day, Jesus got his marching orders from his heavenly Father. When you begin your day, what determines which items on your "to do" list will get top priority? What could you do today that would increase the chance that you'd pray first thing tomorrow morning, letting God guide your priorities?

Notes

My concrete resolution from this session:

Closing prayer:

Dear God, I really want to be closer to you, but I can see all sorts of things that get in the way. Even with the best of intentions, I'm all too aware of all the ways in which I fall short. Thank you for accepting me as I am, and delighting in my desire to grow. Even when I fail, your love for me stays steadfast. Where I am weak, you are strong. Be my strength as I seek to become more purposeful in the way I live. I need you. Amen.

If you are going through these questions in a small group, I encourage you to take time to share specific prayer requests. It'll build trust and greater depth in your friendships as you give one another the gift of revealing the areas where you need God's help. Pray for one another during the time between sessions. God is "able to accomplish far more than all we ask or imagine!" Ephesians 3:20.

SESSION 2

STOP STRIVING AND REST

*Read Section Two: Putting Your Priorities in Order
and Priority One: Your Relationship with God*

1. With all the opportunities and freedoms that women experience today, it can be hard to decide which are the best choices to make. So many things call out for our time and attention. What are the "hot spots" or stress points in your life? If you could live more purposefully in one key area, which one would it be?

2. Priority One is your relationship with God. One of the obstacles to putting God first is the belief that following him is just a bunch of rules to obey. Nothing could be further from the truth. What God wants is a love relationship with each one of us. What insight do the following verses give in terms of God's love for us?

Psalm 86:15, "But you, O Lord, are a God merciful and gracious, slow to anger and abounding in steadfast love and faithfulness."

Romans 8:38-39, "For I am convinced that neither death, nor life, nor angels, nor principalities, nor present things, nor future things, nor powers, nor height, nor depth, nor any other creature will be able to separate us from the love of God in Christ Jesus our Lord."

Zephaniah 3:17, "The LORD your God is in your midst, a mighty one who will save; he will rejoice over you with gladness; he will quiet you by his love; he will exult over you with loud singing."

"Our doubts do not destroy God's love, nor does our faith create it. It originates in the very nature of God, who is love, and it flows to us through our union with his blessed son." Jerry Bridges

3. Why does God deserve to be our first priority?

4. In Priority 1: Your Relationship with God, Lisa shared Steve Allgeyer's teaching about Harold and the Purple crayon. We were challenged to think about what we would draw with our purple crayons, which is basically the picture in our minds of the best circumstances possible. Whatever it is that we want so badly, dream about, and are working to achieve, God asks us to offer to him. Surrendering the purple crayon doesn't mean that we cease to have an opinion or that we give up and let our dreams die. It means that we offer to God what is most precious to us, and tell him we trust him to allow whatever he knows is ultimately best for us. Where is your purple crayon? Is it tightly wrapped in your fist? Does God have it? Have you offered it to him, but taken it back when circumstances became difficult?

Notes

5. Sometimes we just feel too tired and weary to put God first. It sounds like a lot of effort, and all we want is a little fun or some rest. When we feel this way, we're failing to recognize that when we put God first, he replenishes us in a way that nothing else can. Read the following verses and paraphrase in your own words the promises God has made to us for those times when we're worn out and depleted.

Isaiah 40:29-31, "He gives power to the faint, abundant strength to the weak. Though young men faint and grow weary, and youths stagger and fall, they that hope in the LORD will renew their strength, they will soar on eagles' wings; they will run and not grow weary, walk and not grow faint."

Philippians 4:13, "I can do all things through Christ who strengthens me."

2 Corinthians 12:10, "But he said to me, 'My grace is sufficient for you, for my power is made perfect in weakness.' Therefore I will boast all the more gladly about my weaknesses, so that Christ's power may rest on me."

6. Circle any of the following things that have kept you from making God the highest priority in your life.

I've thought he just wanted me to follow rules.

I've struggled to trust God.

I've been weary.

I've been disappointed with what life has dealt me, and it's made it hard for me to open my heart to God.

I've been so busy- I've loved God in my heart, but failed to love Him in my schedule.

God understands. He knows how you have struggled. Every day, he offers you a fresh start. He asks you to trust him—to give him the benefit of the doubt, recognizing that he's got the big picture, while we do not. The first step towards making God the highest priority in your life is committing to give him what is really precious, your time. Could you choose a time of the day for the next week that you will protect for God? Ask him to help you to stay faithful to your appointment with him. Put it on your calendar, just like you would for any other commitment.

The time of day that I'm committing to God this week is:

_____

My concrete resolution from this session:

Closing prayer:

Dear God, It's hard for me to sort through things that I've thought about you and sometimes blamed you for, and reconcile them with the way you are revealed in Scripture. Help me to get to know you. Not the God of my imagination. The real you. Please fix my faulty thinking. Help me to give the best of my day to you—not just the leftovers. I get busy and think I don't have time to pray. Help me to remember that if I'll put you first, you'll take care of all the details of my life. I've tried so hard to keep everything under control. I want you to be the one keeping it all together. Please help me. Amen.

HOPE FOR YOUR MARRIAGE

*Read Priority Two: Tending to Your Heart
and Priority Three: Your Marriage*

*If we can apply the lessons from Priority Two: Tending to Your Heart,
we'll have taken big strides forward in strengthening our marriages.
If we just read the chapter, thinking the information is interesting, but
we don't actually put into practice what we've learned, we'll come
to our spouse with needs he can't possibly meet. He'll be guaranteed
to disappoint. When our hearts are filled up with God's love, it can
overflow into our relationships. When we feel we lack love in our
marriages, God's love can spill out of our hearts, bringing transforma-
tion and hope.*

1. What are some of the ways that God has shown you His love
for you? Think of the memories you cherish and moments that
have moved you to tears. They are all gifts sent to you by the
Lover of your soul.

2. Have you experienced unconditional love in any of your earthly relationships? How does the way in which you have been loved affect your ability to truly believe that when God looks at you, He says, "I love you so much. I'll fight for you to the death"?

3. We all come to marriage with expectations. When they aren't met, we are disappointed and sometimes disillusioned. Some of those expectations are fair; others are unrealistic. Read the following quote by Ruth Bell Graham. Have you ever fallen into this pattern in your marriage? Do you agree or disagree that this level of expectation sets a man up for failure? What do we do when our husbands disappoint us?

"It is a foolish woman who expects her husband to be to her that which only Jesus Christ Himself can be: always ready to forgive, totally understanding, unendingly patient, invariably tender and loving, unfailing in every area, anticipating every need, and making more than adequate provision." *Ruth Bell Graham*

"She became my mirror," Peter says of his wife. "She gave ma a new image of myself. Even now, regardless of how I feel, when I look at her she gives me a warm, loving smile that tells me I am ok," he tells confidently.[1]
—*Walking with Purpose,* page 96

4. What kind of a mirror are you? What does your husband see reflected in your face?

5. Have you ever experienced a difficult circumstance in your marriage that drew you closer to Christ? In what way did He help you through the trial?

6. Even when we're trying to do the right things, we can end up in the midst of circumstances that are less than ideal. We might wonder if God wants us to stay in a marriage when we aren't happy. While we may know that God hates divorce (Malachi 2:16), we can't imagine that God would really want us to feel so unfulfilled.

Could it be that there is something more important to God than our comfort levels? By no means am I suggesting that a woman should stay in an abusive marriage. But so often, the issue isn't one of abuse.

What would happen if we changed our focus? The following verses offer truths to chew on and apply during times of dissatisfaction in marriage. Underline and comment on anything that rings true or challenges you.

Matthew 16:24, "Then Jesus said to his disciples, 'Whoever wishes to come after me must deny himself, take up his cross, and follow me.'"

Romans 3:10, "All have sinned and fall short of the glory of God." No one is perfect.

Romans 12:21, "Do not be overcome by evil, but overcome evil with good."

Proverbs 15:1, "A mild answer turns back wrath, but a harsh word stirs up anger."

1 Peter 5:8, "Your opponent the devil is prowling around like a roaring lion looking for someone to devour." Remember who the real enemy is.

My concrete resolution from this session:

Closing prayer:

Dear God, It's a little mind boggling for me to think that you have a place in your heart for me. Thank you for loving me unconditionally. You want the same thing I want- to be loved. Help me to love you back. I know I love imperfectly, but as your love fills my heart, I pray it'll spill over into the lives of the people around me. Help me to let go of the need to be right. Help me to resist the temptation to settle for a "good enough" marriage. Help me to not just focus on the ways I want my husband to change. Change me. Amen.

SESSION

4

REACH YOUR CHILD'S HEART

Read Priority Four: Reaching Your Child's Heart

1. Have you experienced the difference between disciplining children for outward behavior and disciplining to reach the heart?

2. What are ways that we can continue to reach our children spiritually when they have reached an age when their peers are their greatest influence?

3. What are your goals for your children? To help in determining your goals, think about your vision for the kind of man or woman you'd like your child to grow up to be. (Goals could be academic, spiritual, physical, emotional...). After listing your goals for each child, circle each goal that has eternal value.

4. What activities and priorities are most likely to get in the way of you taking the time to give your children spiritual guidance and nurture? Are there any things in your family life that need to be removed or pared back?

5. Our children aren't just learning from what we say, they are observing how we act. How do the following verses challenge you as a mother?

Proverbs 14:1, "The wise woman builds her house, but with her own hands the foolish one tears hers down."

1 Peter 3:3-4, "Your beauty should not come from outward adornment, such as elaborate hairstyles and the wearing of gold jewelry or fine clothes. Rather, it should be that of your inner self, the unfading beauty of a gentle and quiet spirit, which is of great worth in God's sight."

Colossians 3:12-15, "Put on then, as God's chosen ones, holy and beloved, heartfelt compassion, kindness, humility, gentleness, and patience, bearing with one another and forgiving one another...and over all these put on love, that is, the bond of perfection. And let the peace of Christ control your hearts, the peace into which you were also called in one body. And be thankful."

6. While some seasons of motherhood are fulfilling and full of joy, others can also be exhausting and discouraging. Underline portions of the following verses that you find encouraging. Write your favorite of the verses on an index card to carry with you.

Jeremiah 29:11, "'For I know the plans I have for you,' declares the LORD, 'plans to prosper you and not to harm you, plans to give you hope and a future.'"

Psalm 37:23-24, "The Lord makes firm the steps of the one who delights in him. Though he may stumble, he will not fall, for the Lord upholds him with his hand."

Ephesians 4:20, "Now all glory to God, who is able, through his mighty power at work within us, to accomplish infinitely more than we might ask or think."

Philippians 4:13, "I have the strength for everything through him who empowers me."

1 Peter 5:7, "Cast all your worries on [God] because he cares for you."

In times of discouragement as mothers, we need to always remember that God can bring something beautiful from the ashes of our lives. God's timing is not like ours. It's never too late for Him. Be comforted by the following words of John Henry Jowett:

> And even supposing we have made mistakes, and we would dearly like to have the choice back again that we might take the other turning, what then? Who is our God? And what are His name and character? Cannot He knit up the raveled bit of work, and in His own infinitely gracious way make it whole again? With all our mistakes we may throw ourselves upon His inexhaustible goodness, and say with St. Teresa, "Undertake Thou for me, O Lord."
>
> It is the very gospel of His grace that He can repair the things that are broken. He can reset the joints of the bruised reed. He can restore the broken heart. He can deal with the broken vow. And if He can do all this, can He not deal with our mistakes? If unknowingly we went astray and took the wrong turning, will not His infinite love correct our mistakes, and make the crooked straight?[2]

My concrete resolution from this session:

Closing prayer:

Dear God, Help me to have your perspective on the importance of my role as a mother. It's so easy to get caught up in what everyone around me says about raising children. Help me to care most about the things that are important to you. In five, ten or twenty years, what will I wish that I'd done differently today? Help me to mother in a purposeful way. I know that no matter how hard I try, I won't be a perfect mother. For all the times when I fall short, I thank you for your grace. Thank you for your infinite love that draws straight with crooked lines. Amen.

SESSION
5

A CALMER HOME
AND DEEPER FRIENDSHIPS

Read Priority Five: Clarity in the Clutter of
Your Home and Priority Six: Friendship

1. The first step in sorting through the clutter in our lives has to do with preparing our hearts. What insight can be gained from the following verses as we seek to start each day with the right attitude?

Psalm 101:2, "I will walk in my house with blameless heart." (It can be easy to behave one way out in public, but get a little ugly in private. This verse challenges us to treat those at home with the same grace that we give the people outside our front doors.)

Colossians 3:23-24, "Whatever you do, work heartily, as for the Lord and not for men, knowing that from the Lord you will receive the inheritance as your reward. You are serving the Lord Christ."

Luke 6:38, "Give and it will be given to you. Good measure, pressed down, shaken together, running over, will be put into your lap."

2. It can be overwhelming to start the process of bringing more order to our homes. The enormity of the task tempts us to say, "I can't! It's too much work. I give up!" Instead of trying to tackle everything all at once, it's wise to start with baby steps. Identify the area in your home that is causing you the most frustration (meal preparation, money management, clutter control, no time taken to rest...). Set a small, realistic goal in that area. Record it here. Ask someone to hold you accountable as you determine to achieve this one goal this week.

My realistic goal for this week:

The person I'll ask to hold me accountable:

As you feel encouraged by the meeting of this one goal and it is beginning to be formed into a habit, add another small, realistic goal to your schedule. "That which we persist in doing becomes easier- not that the nature of the task has changed, but our ability to do has increased." -Ralph Waldo Emerson

3. Because I can always find something I'd rather do than clean and organize my home, I have posted Bible verses in various places to remind me to keep focused. A verse in the kitchen reads, "Better a dry morsel with quietness than a house full of feasting with strife," Proverbs 17:1. Another near the hooks for coats and baskets for mittens says, "Let all things be done decently and in good order," 1 Corinthians 14:40. Which of the following verses and motivate you? Circle your favorite, and consider writing it out as a reminder and strategically placing it somewhere in your house.

Colossians 3:23, "Whatever you do, do from the heart, as for the Lord and not for others."

Galatians 6:9 "Let us not become weary in doing good, for at the proper time we will reap a harvest if we do not give up."

Psalm 141:3 "Set a guard, O Lord, over my mouth; keep watch over the door of my lips."

Proverbs 31:25-27 "Strength and honor are her clothing."

Ephesians 4:26 "Do not let the sun go down while you are still angry."

Luke 6:31 "Do to others as you would have them do to you."

> Nothing kills a good friendship like comparison, because it gets in the way of our being happy for one another, and it plants a seed of bitterness in our hearts that chokes out true love for another person.
> —*Walking with Purpose*, page 150

4. Comparing ourselves to others often leads us to feel insecure, and our friendships suffer as a result.

What if we could look at one other through grace-healed eyes? What if we could reflect the verse, "…whatever is true, whatever is noble, whatever is right, whatever is pure, whatever is lovely, whatever is admirable- if anything is excellent or praiseworthy-think about such things," Philippians 4:8? Make a study of one of your closest friends. Do this in order to call out the goodness in her, rather than to compare yourself to her. List her name and best qualities here. Take a concrete step to call out the goodness in her, through a letter, email, or phone call.

Notes

5. A good friend is not self-centered in friendship. She truly seeks the best for the other. How can we balance a servant's heart in friendship with biblical kindness (speaking the truth in love)?

6. Reflect on your "inner circle" of closer friends. Who in your inner circle enriches your life? Why? How does she cause you to grow deeper and become more like Christ?

Proverbs 27:17, "As iron sharpens iron, so one person sharpens another." How can you be that deeper friend to someone?

My concrete resolution from this session:

Closing Prayer:

Dear God, Help me to be other-focused in friendship. Instead of thinking about what I want to get out of my relationships, help me to pour in to the lives of others. I want to be a better friend, and I want to experience deeper friendships. May I become a woman who calls out the goodness in others. As I invest in my friends through the gift of my time, please help these relationships to blossom and grow deeper. Amen.

DISCOVER YOUR PASSION & PURPOSE

*Read Priority Seven: Outside Activities
and Your True Worth*

1. In what area of life are you most tempted to settle for mediocrity when God is asking you to kick it up a notch and experience more of what he has planned for you?

2. If you could help any group of people in the world, who would it be, and what would you do?

3. What woman has most inspired you through her response to her holy discontent?

4. What are some ways we can prevent burn out when serving those in need?

Holiness isn't measured by our perfection. It's measured by how we love. God places great value on generosity, putting others' needs before our own- a mother getting up in the middle of the night with a sick child, a wife who overlooks the raised toilet seat.
—*Walking with Purpose,* page 177

5. The world around us tells us that all sorts of superficial things are important. It's hard to refocus on what God says matters most.

Which of your thoughts need to be renewed? What are the messages that you find yourself dwelling on, the thoughts that pop into your mind and bring you discouragement?

When [my daughter, Amy] got home and shared what had happened with me, I did my best to push aside my own feelings and point her toward truth. I told her that she needed to decide today whose approval she was going to go after. If she was going to pursue the approval of the girls at school- and then whoever else was popular later in her school years- she would probably still be seeking this peer approval when she was forty. That's how it works. When we seek people's approval and make that our focus, our work never ends. The goalposts always seem to shift. But Amy had a choice. She could decide to pursue God's approval. She could decide to live every day making choices that make him happy. I challenged her to decide. Whose approval was she after?

—*Walking with Purpose,* page 181

6. Whose opinion matters most? We start to struggle with this dilemma when we're young, and it often continues into adulthood. It spills into how we parent, and we can inadvertently encourage our children to seek approval in all places that lead to a never ending quest to measure up.

Whose approval are you after? The world's approval will be fickle, and the goal posts will continually shift. Seeking God's approval is very different. What insights do you gain from the following verses?

Hosea 11:4, "I led them with cords of human kindness, with ties of love; I lifted the yoke from their neck and bent down to feed them."

Galatians 1:10, "Am I now trying to win the approval of human beings, or of God? Or am I trying to please people? If I were still trying to please people, I would not be a servant of Christ."

My concrete resolution from this session:

Closing Prayer:

Dear God, I've spent a lot of time and energy trying to earn the approval of people. Sometimes it's earned me what I wanted, but other times it has seemed that I'll just never be good enough. Help me to desire your approval more than that of any person. I'm ready to trade in my old way of measuring my worth. Thank you for loving me unconditionally. Thank you for measuring my worth at the cross, and considering me worth the greatest sacrifice. What can I give in return for such a gift? I give you my heart. Amen.

END NOTES

1. Dennis Rainey and Barbara Rainey, *The New Building Your Mate's Self-Esteem* (Nashville, TN: Thomas Nelson, 1995) 3-4.

2. Jean Fleming, *A Mother's Heart* (Colorado Springs, CO: NavPress, 1982), page 41.

Made in the USA
San Bernardino, CA
17 July 2015